Teach Your Dog

SPANISH

Funny & surprisingly clever books. Love. Love.
DAWN FRENCH, ACTOR & COMEDIAN

Anne Cakebread not only has the best name in the Universe, she has also come up with a brilliantly fun book which will help humans and canines learn new languages.
RICHARD HERRING, COMEDIAN

People are crackers, mate. They think you can teach dogs Spanish, when we all know they only speak French.
ARTHUR SMITH, WRITER & COMEDIAN

Teach Your Dog

SPANISH

Anne Cakebread

Thank you to:
Helen, Marcie, Lily and Nina,
my family, friends and neighbours in
St Dogmaels for all their support and
encouragement, Carolyn at Y Lolfa, and
Martha Lloyd Morgan, Thomas Bunstead and
María José Rancaño Bambach for Spanish
translations and pronunciations.
Gracias.

In memory of Frieda, who started us on
the *Teach Your Dog* journey.

First impression 2021

© Anne Cakebread & Y Lolfa Cyf., 2021
This book is subject to copyright and may not be reproduced by any
means except for review purposes without the prior written consent of
the publishers.

Illustrations and design by Anne Cakebread

ISBN: 978-1-80099-033-3

Published and printed in Wales on paper from well-maintained
forests by Y Lolfa Cyf., Talybont, Ceredigion, SY24 5HE Wales
e-mail ylolfa@ylolfa.com
website www.ylolfa.com
tel +44 1970 832 304
fax +44 1970 832 782

I grew up only speaking English.
When I moved to west Wales, I adopted Frieda,
a rescue whippet, who would only obey
Welsh commands.
Slowly, whilst dealing with Frieda, I realised that I was
overcoming my nerves about speaking Welsh aloud,
and my Welsh was improving as a result
– this gave me the idea of creating a series of books
to help others learn.
You don't even have to go to abroad to practise.
If you haven't got a dog, any pet or soft toy will do:
just have fun learning and speaking a new language.

– Anne Cakebread

"Hello"

"Hola"

pron:
"**O-la**"

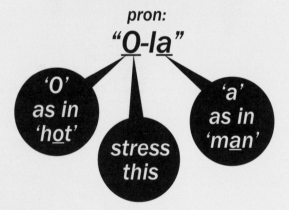

'O'
as in
'h<u>o</u>t'

stress
this

'a'
as in
'm<u>a</u>n'

"Come here"

"Ven aquí"

pron:
"Ben <u>a</u>-<u>key</u>"

'a'
as in
'm<u>a</u>n'

stress
this

"Do you want a cuddle?"

"¿Quieres un abrazo?"

pron:

"Key-e-ress oon abra-tho?"

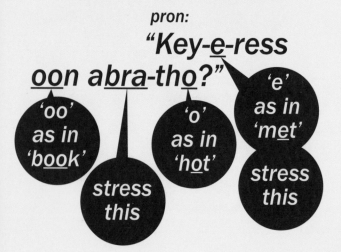

'oo' as in '<u>book</u>'

stress this

'o' as in 'h<u>o</u>t'

'e' as in 'm<u>e</u>t'

stress this

"Well done!"

"¡Bien hecho!"

pron:
"Be-yen <u>etch</u>-o!"

'e' as in 'm<u>e</u>t'

'o' as in 'h<u>o</u>t'

stress this

"Fetch!"

"¡Trae!"

pron:

"Tra-e!"

'a'
as in
'man'

'e'
as in
'met'

"Leave it!"

"¡Déjalo!"

pron:

"De-cha-lo!"

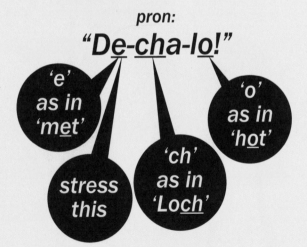

'e'
as in
'met'

stress
this

'ch'
as in
'Loch'

'o'
as in
'hot'

"Sit!"

"¡Siéntate!"

pron:

"See-<u>en</u>-t<u>a</u>-t<u>e</u>!"

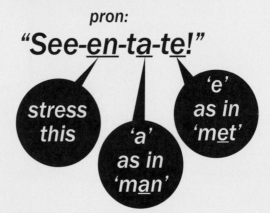

stress
this

'a'
as in
'm<u>a</u>n'

'e'
as in
'm<u>e</u>t'

"No!"

"¡No!"

pron:
"N<u>o</u>!"

'o'
as in
'h<u>o</u>t'

"Stay!"

"¡Quieto!"

pron:

"Key-e-to!"

'e'
as in
'met'

'o'
as in
'hot'

stress
this

"Bathtime"

"Hora del baño"

pron:
"<u>O</u>-r<u>a</u> del bany<u>o</u>"

'o'
as in
'h<u>o</u>t'

'a'
as in
'm<u>a</u>n'

'o'
as in
'h<u>o</u>t'

"Bedtime"

"Hora de acostarse"

pron:

"O-ra de a-coss-tar-se"

'O'
as in
'hot'

'a'
as in
'man'

'e'
as in
'met'

"Lunchtime"

"Hora de comer"

pron:

"O-ra de co-mehr"

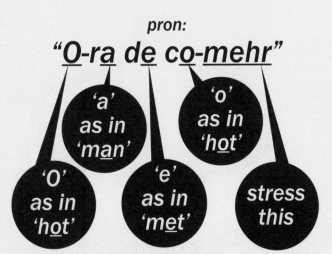

'a' as in 'man'

'o' as in 'hot'

'O' as in 'hot'

'e' as in 'met'

stress this

"Are you full?"

"¿Estás lleno?"

pron:

"Ess-tass ye-no?"

stress this

'e' as in 'met'

'o' as in 'hot'

"All gone"

"Se acabó"

pron:

"Se akka-bo"

'e' as in 'met'

stress this

'o' as in 'hot'

"Good morning"

"Buenos días"

pron:

"Bwenoss dee-ass"

stress
this

"Goodnight"

"Buenas noches"

pron:
"Bwenass <u>no</u>-chess"

stress
this

'o'
as in
'h<u>o</u>t'

"Don't scratch"

"No te rasques"

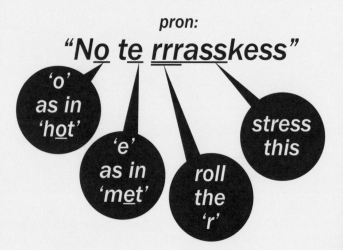

"Let's go!"

"¡Vamos!"

pron:

"<u>Ba</u>-moss!"

stress this

'a' as in 'm<u>a</u>n'

"Up you go!"

"¡Arriba!"

pron:

"A-rrree-ba!"

'A' as in 'man'

roll the 'r'

stress this

'a' as in 'man'

"Go straight ahead"

"Sigue recto"

pron:

"<u>See</u>-g<u>e</u> <u>rrr</u>eck-t<u>o</u>"

stress this

'e' as in 'm<u>e</u>t'

roll the 'r'

'o' as in 'h<u>o</u>t'

"Turn left"

"Gira a
la izquierda"

pron:
"Hee-ra a la
ith-key-air-da"

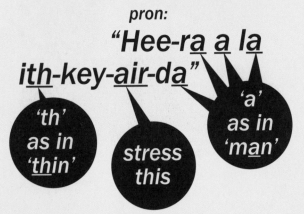

'th'
as in
'thin'

stress
this

'a'
as in
'man'

"Turn right"

"Gira a la derecha"

pron:

"Hee-ra a la de-re-cha"

'a' as in 'man'

'e' as in 'met'

'cha' as in 'chat'

stress this

"Take care"

"Cuídate"

pron:
"Kwee-<u>da</u>-t<u>e</u>"

stress
this

'a'
as in
'm<u>a</u>n'

'e'
as in
'm<u>e</u>t'

"What's up?"

"¿Qué pasa?"

pron:
"Ke pa-sa?"

'e'
as in
'met'

'a'
as in
'man'

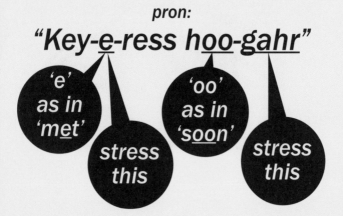

"Lie down!"

"¡Echate!"

pron:
"*Etch-a-te!*"

stress this

'a' as in 'm<u>a</u>n'

'e' as in 'm<u>e</u>t'

"Say 'please'!"

"¡Di 'por favor'!"

pron:

"Dee 'por fa-bore'!"

'a'
as in
'man'

stress
this

"Can I have the ball?"

"¿Me das la pelota?"

pron:

"Me dass la pellotta?"

stress this

stress this

'e' as in 'met'

'a' as in 'man'

'a' as in 'man'

"Please can I have some churros and chocolate?"

"Por favor, ¿me das churros y chocolate?"

pron:

"Por fa-bore, me dass choorrros ee choko-latt-e?"

roll the 'r'

'e' as in 'met'

'o as in 'hot'

'e' as in 'met'

"Very clever"

"Muy listo"

pron:
"Moo-ee lees-to"

stress
this

'o'
as in
'hot'

"It's snowing"

"Está nevando"

pron:

"Ess-ta nebando"

'a' as in 'man'

stress this

'o' as in 'hot'

"It's cold"

"Hace frío"

pron:

"Ath-e free-o"

'A' as in 'man'

'e' as in 'met'

stress this

'o' as in 'hot'

"It's hot"

"Hace calor"

pron:
"Ath-e ka-lohr"

'A'
as in
'man'

'e'
as in
'met'

'a'
as in
'man'

stress
this

"It's raining"

"Está lloviendo"

pron:

"Ess-<u>ta</u> yo-bee-<u>end</u>-o"

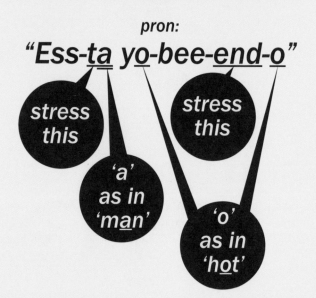

stress this

stress this

'a' as in 'm<u>a</u>n'

'o' as in 'h<u>o</u>t'

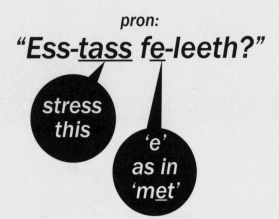

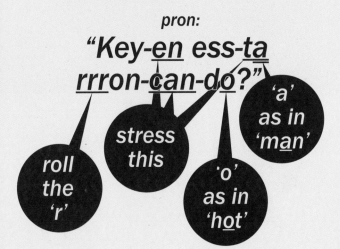

"Have you got enough room?"

"¿Tienes espacio suficiente?"

stress this

'a' as in 'man'

'o' as in 'hot'

pron:

"Tee-eneess ess-pa-theo soo-fee-thee-en-te?"

'th' as in 'thin'

stress this

'e' as in met'

"I won't be long"

"No tardaré mucho"

pron:

"No tar-dar-e moo-cho"

'o' as in 'hot'

'e' as in 'met'

stress this

'o' as in 'hot'

"Be quiet!"

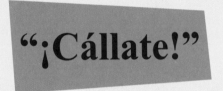

"¡Cállate!"

pron:

"Ka-ya-te!"

stress this

'a' as in 'man'

'e' as in 'met'

"Who did that?"

"¿Quién hizo eso?"

pron:

"Key-en _eeth-o_ ess_o_?"

stress this

'o' as in 'h_o_t'

"There's a queue
for the loo"

"Hay una cola
para el baño"

pron:

"Eye oon<u>a</u> koll<u>a</u>
p<u>a</u>r<u>a</u> el ban-y<u>o</u>"

'a'
as in
'm<u>a</u>n'

'a'
as in
'm<u>a</u>n'

'o'
as in
'h<u>o</u>t'

1

"uno"

pron:

"oo-no"

stress this

'o' as in 'hot'

2

"dos"

pron:

"doss"

3

"tres"

pron:
"tress"

4

"cuatro"

pron:
"<u>kwa-tro</u>"

'o'
as in
'h<u>o</u>t'

**stress
this**

5

"cinco"

pron:

"thing-ko"

'o'
as in
'hot'

6

"seis"

pron:

"say-ss"

"Thank you"

"Gracias"

pron:

"Gra-thee-ass"

stress this

'a' as in 'man'

'th' as in 'thin'

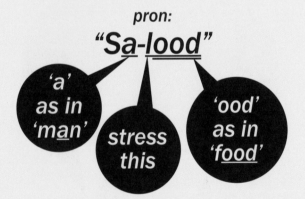

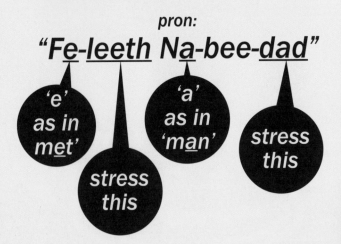

"Congratulations!"

"¡Felicidades!"

pron:

"F<u>e</u>-leeth-ee-dad-ess!"

'e' as in m<u>e</u>t'

"Happy Birthday"

"Feliz Cumpleaños"

pron:
"Fe-leeth Coom-ple-ann-yoss"

'oo'
as in
'book'

'e'
as in
met'

"I love you"

"Te quiero"

pron:
"Te key-air-o"

'e'
as in
m<u>e</u>t'

'o'
as in
'h<u>o</u>t'

"Goodbye"

"Adiós"

pron:
"Addy-oss"

stress
this